THE POETRY OF RAILWAYS

Frontispiece: 'Danger Ahead!'

The
Poetry of
Railways

edited by Samuel Carr

B. T. Batsford Ltd, London

To Sir John Betjeman

First published 1978
Copyright S. Carr 1978

ISBN 0 7134 0222 9

Designed by Alan Hamp
Filmset in 12 on 13 pt Monophoto Bembo
by Keyspools Ltd, Golborne, Lancs.
Printed in Great Britain by Butler & Tanner Ltd, Frome
for the publishers, B.T.Batsford Ltd,
4 Fitzhardinge Street, London W1H0AH

Contents

The front endpaper is of a Great Northern 515 'Consolidation' type, reproduced from John H. White Jr., *Early American Locomotives* (Dover Publications, 1972). The back endpaper is from Clarance P. Hornung, *Handbook of Early Advertising Art*, 1947 (Dover Publications)

The Illustrations

8

Introduction

Poetry about trains may be doggerel, it may be the work of geniuses like Thomas Hardy or Giosuè Carducci, but, thanks to its subject, it is seldom uninteresting. The greater the poem, however, the more likely it is to be concerned with a particular situation ('Midnight on the Great Western') or with the poet's state of mind ('*Alla Stazione*') than with the railway itself. Those with their eyes steadily on the train will more probably be writing at the level of William McGonagall's 'The Newport Railway' than of W.H. Auden's 'The Night Mail'.

Much railway poetry was composed for recitation. This was certainly the case with the anonymous ballads which, in America more than in Europe, came to form part of folk literature. In England these recitation pieces usually had an acknowledged author – and as often as not his name was Alexander Anderson (1845–1909). Anderson had worked as a surfaceman on the G. & S.W.R., so 'Jim Whistle', 'Behind Time', 'Nottman' and the other poems in *Songs of the Rail* were written from first-hand experience. (Later, it might be added in parenthesis, Anderson left the railway to become Librarian at Edinburgh University: a job where, whether or not through cause and effect, he was neither conspicuously successful nor uniformly sober).

Why, it might be asked, include a prose passage in a verse anthology. One answer is that Dickens often *was* a poet in his imaginative imagery (if less so because what he wrote sometimes unintentionally scans). Another is that the quotation from *Dombey and Son* creates so graphic a picture that one would be sorry to leave it out. That Dickens was himself much excited by the railway in its apogee (the date is 1846) is shown both by the actuality of the description and by the fact that it was written from vivid recollection in Switzerland.

For the artist, the train figures more often as a detail in a

9

landscape (Pissarro), for the atmosphere it creates (Turner, Monet, Manet) or for its passengers (Daumier) than for its own sake. The cuttings and viaducts which sometimes appear in Cézanne landscapes never include a train. But just as the achievements of the railway engineers were often superior to those of the architects proper, so the work of the engineering draughtsmen in publications like Daniel Kinnear Clark's *Railway Machinery* (1855) was aesthetically an improvement on that of their Royal Academy contemporaries, such as Robert Musgrave Joy, Abraham Solomon and W.P. Frith, who also portrayed the railway scene. In a comparable but parallel way, the cosy falsification of the Currier and Ives prints is more acceptable than that of the English high-art painters in the railway genre.

Not only the American popular artists, but the more serious ones too were better able to come to terms with the age of steam than were most of their European contemporaries. As some of the illustrations in this collection show, George Inness in the last century and Joseph Pickett, Edward Hopper and Ben Shahn in this, treated railway themes with uncondescending straightforwardness. The pity is that other great American artists like George Bellows, Winslow Homer and Thomas Eakins, all of them concerned with the contemporary scene, were apparently not interested in doing so.

As to the photographs, it might well be asked why these, which are superficially so factual and prosaic, are in the same book as the verse and the pictures. The reason is that old photographs also have their poetry. Whether this is always the intention of their photographers, or whether it comes with the poor focus and grainy quality of many old photographs, is a question hard to answer. Whatever the explanation, there can be no doubt that Victorian photographs often leave the imagination freedom to roam and so, like paintings, drawings and prints, may provide appropriate counterparts to the poems.

Artists and poets alike seemed often to have an imperfect understanding of the mechanics of railway travel. Tennyson's often quoted 'ringing grooves of change' (indicating, or so it is said, that he thought the wheels were somehow slotted into grooves) is only one instance of miscomprehension out of many. Both poets and artists, however, at whatever level they worked, generally succeeded in their aim of giving pleasure. Such, too, is the hope of the editor of this collection.

'Matlock Bath from the Station'

Midnight on the Great Western

In the third-class seat sat the journeying boy,
    And the roof-lamp's oily flame
Played down on his listless form and face,
Bewrapt past knowing to what he was going,
    Or whence he came.

In the band of his hat the journeying boy
    Had a ticket stuck; and a string
Around his neck bore the key of his box,
That twinkled gleams of the lamp's sad beam
    Like a living thing.

What past can be yours, O journeying boy
    Towards a world unknown,
Who calmly, as if incurious quite
On all at stake, can undertake
    This plunge alone?

Knows your soul a sphere, O journeying boy,
    Our rude realms far above,
Whence with spacious vision you mark and mete
This region of sin that you find you in,
    But are not of?

THOMAS HARDY (1840–1928)

Wild Engine

from: Journey

Oh the wild engine! Every time I sit
In a train I must remember it.
The way it smashes through the air; its great
Petulant majesty and terrible rate:
Driving the ground before it, with those round
Feet pounding, beating, covering the ground;
The piston using up the white steam so
You cannot watch it when it come or go;
The cutting, the embankment; how it takes
The tunnels, and the clatter that it makes;
So careful of the train and of the track,
Guiding us out, or helping us go back;
Breasting its destination: at the close
Yawning, and slowly dropping to a doze.

HAROLD MONRO (1879–1932)

'A London and North Western Passenger Locomotive'

The Locomotive

Hurrah for the mighty engine;
As he bounds along his track;
Hurrah, for the life that is in him,
And his breath so thick and black.
And hurrah for our fellows, who in their need
Could fashion a thing like him—
With a heart of fire, and a soul of steel
And a Samson in every limb.

ALEXANDER ANDERSON (1845–1909)

Workin' on the railway

In eighteen hundred and forty one,
I put me cord'roy breeches on,
I put me cord'roy breeches on
To work upon the railway.

In eighteen hundred and forty-two
I left the ould world for the new,
Bad cess to the luck that brought me through
To work upon the railroad.

When we left Ireland to come here,
And spend our latter days in cheer,
Our bosses, they did drink strong beer
And Pat worked on the railway.

Our boss's name, it was Tom King,
He kept a store to rob the men,
A Yankee clerk with ink and pen,
To cheat Pat on the railroad.

It's 'Pat do this' and 'Pat do that,'
Without a stocking or cravat,
And nothing but an old straw hat
While Pat works on the railroad.

One Monday morning to our surprise,
Just a half an hour before sunrise,
The dirty divil went to the skies
And Pat worked on the railroad.

And when Pat lays him down to sleep,
The wirey bugs around him creep
And divil a bit can poor Pat sleep,
While he works on the railroad.

'Scotts Run, West Virginia'. *Ben Shahn*

In eighteen hundred and forty-three
'Twas then I met Miss Biddy MacGhee
And an illygant wife she's been to me,
While workin' on the railway.

In eighteen hundred and forty-seven,
Sweet Biddy MacGhee, she went to heaven,
If she left one child, she left eleven,
To work upon the railway.

In eighteen hundred and forty-eight,
I learned to take my whiskey straight,
'Tis an illygant drink and can't be bate
For working on the railway.

ANONYMOUS

To a locomotive in Winter

Thee for my recitative,
Thee in the driving storm even as now, the snow, the winter-
    day declining
Thee in thy panoply, thy measur'd dual throbbing and thy beat
    convulsive,
Thy black cylindric body, golden brass and silvery steel,
Thy ponderous side-bars, parallel and connecting rods,
    gyrating, shuttling at thy sides,
Thy metrical, now swelling pant and roar, now tapering in the
    distance,
Thy great protruding head-light fix'd in front,
Thy long, pale, floating vapour-pennants, tinged with delicate
    purple,
The dense and murky clouds out-belching from thy smoke-
    stack,
Thy knitted frame, thy springs and valves, the tremulous
    twinkle of thy wheels,
Thy train of cars behind, obedient, merrily following,
Through gale or calm, now swift, now slack, yet steadily
    careering;
Type of the modern—emblem of motion and power—pulse of
    the continent,
For once come serve the Muse and merge in verse, even as here I
    see thee,
With storm and buffeting gusts of wind and falling snow,
By day thy warning ringing bell to sound its notes,
By night thy silent signal lamps to swing.

Fierce-throated beauty!
Roll through my chant with all thy lawless music, thy swinging
    lamps at night,
Thy madly-whistled laughter, echoing, rumbling like an
    earthquake, rousing all,
Law of thyself complete, thine own track firmly holding,

'Snowbound'. *From a Currier and Ives lithograph*

(No sweetness debonair of tearful harp or glib piano thine,)
Thy trills of shrieks by rocks and hills return'd,
Launch'd o'er the prairies wide, across the lakes,
To the free skies unpent and glad and strong.

WALT WHITMAN (1819–1892)

The Tay Bridge disaster

Beautiful Railway Bridge of the Silv'ry Tay!
Alas! I am very sorry to say
That ninety lives have been taken away
On the last Sabbath day of 1879,
Which will be remember'd for a very long time.

'Twas about seven o'clock at night,
And the wind it blew with all its might,
And the rain came pouring down,
And the dark clouds seem'd to frown,
And the Demon of the Air seem'd to say—
'I'll blow down the Bridge of Tay.'

When the train left Edinburgh
The passengers' hearts were light and felt no sorrow,
But Boreas blew a terrific gale,
Which made their hearts for to quail,
And many of the passengers with fear did say—
'I hope God will send us safe across the Bridge of Tay.'

But when the train came near to Wormit Bay,
Boreas he did loud and angry bray,
And shook the central girders of the Bridge of Tay
On the last Sabbath day of 1879,
Which will be remember'd for a very long time.

So the train sped on with all its might,
And Bonnie Dundee soon hove in sight,
And the passengers' hearts felt light,
Thinking they would enjoy themselves on the New Year,
With their friends at home they lov'd most dear,
And wish them all a happy New Year.

So the train mov'd slowly along the Bridge of Tay,

'The Tay Bridge Disaster'. *From an engraving after F. Dodd*

Until it was about midway,
Then the central girders with a crash gave way,
And down went the train and passengers into the Tay!
The Storm Fiend did loudly bray,
Because ninety lives had been taken away,
On the last Sabbath day of 1879,
Which will be remember'd for a very long time.

As soon as the catastrophe came to be known
The alarm from mouth to mouth was blown,
And the cry rang out all o'er the town,
Good Heavens! the Tay Bridge is blown down,
And a passenger train from Edinburgh,
Which fill'd all the people's hearts with sorrow,
And made them for to turn pale,
Because none of the passengers were sav'd to tell the tale
How the disaster happen'd on the last Sabbath day of 1879
Which will be remember'd for a very long time.

It must have been an awful sight,
To witness in the dusky moonlight,
While the Storm Fiend did laugh, and angry did bray,
Along the Railway Bridge of the Silv'ry Tay.
Oh! ill-fated Bridge of the Silv'ry Tay,
I must now conclude my lay
By telling the world fearlessly without the least dismay,
That your central girders would not have given way,
At least many sensible men do say,
Had they been supported on each side with buttresses,
At least many sensible men confesses,
For the stronger we our houses do build,
The less chance we have of being killed.

WILLIAM MCGONAGALL (1830–1902)

The Lackawanna Railroad

The Lackawanna Railroad where does it go?
It goes from Jersey City to Buffalo.
Some of the trains stop at Maysville but they are few
Most of them go right through
Except the 8.22
Going west but the 10.12 bound for Jersey City
That is the train we like the best
As it takes you to Jersey City
Where you can take a ferry or tube for New York City.
The Lackawanna runs many freights
Sometimes they run late
But that does not make so much difference with a freight
Except the people who have to wait for their freight
Maysville people patronise the Interurban aspecialty the
     farmers
So the Interurban cuts into the business of the Lackawanna,
But if you are going to New York City or Buffalo
The Lackawanna is the way to go.
Will say in conclusion that we consider it an honor
That the City of Maysville is on the Lackawanna.

STEPHEN GALE

'The Lackawanna Valley'. *George Inness*

A trip to Paris and Belgium

London to Folkestone

A constant keeping-past of shaken trees,
And a bewildered glitter of loose road;
Banks of bright growth, with single blades atop
Against white sky: and wires—a constant chain—
That seem to draw the clouds along with them
(Things which one stoops against the light to see
Through the low window; shaking by at rest,
Or fierce like water as the swiftness grows);
And, seen through fences or a bridge far off,
Trees that in moving keep their intervals
Still one 'twixt bar and bar; and then at times
Long reaches of green level, where one cow,
Feeding among her fellows that feed on,
Lifts her slow neck, and gazes for the sound.

Fields mown in ridges; and close garden-crops
Of the earth's increase; and a constant sky
Still with clear trees that let you see the wind;
And snatches of the engine-smoke, by fits
Tossed to the wind against the landscape, where
Rooks stooping heave their wings upon the day.

Brick walls we pass between, passed so at once
That for the suddenness I cannot know
Or what, or where begun, or where at end.
Sometimes a station in grey quite; whence,
With a short gathered champing of pent sound,
We are let out upon the air again.
Pauses of water soon, at intervals,
That has the sky in it;—the reflexes
O' the trees move towards the bank as we go by,
Leaving the water's surface plain. I now
Lie back and close my eyes a space; for they
Smart from the open forwardness of thought
Fronting the wind.

★   ★   ★

'Le Wagon de troisième Classe'. *Honoré Daumier*

          I did not scribble more,
Be certain, after this; but yawned, and read,
And nearly dozed a little, I believe;
Till, stretching up against the carriage-back,
I was roused altogether, and looked out
To where the pale sea brooded murmuring.

   Boulogne to Amiens and Paris

   Strong extreme speed, that the brain hurries with,
Further than trees, and hedges, and green grass
Whitened by distance,—further than small pools
Held among fields and gardens, further than
Haystacks, and wind-mill-sails, and roofs and herds,—
The sea's last margin ceases at the sun.

25

The sea has left us, but the sun remains.
Sometimes the country spreads aloof in tracts
Smooth from the harvest; sometimes sky and land
Are shut from the square space the window leaves
By a dense crowd of trees, stem behind stem
Passing across each other as we pass:
Sometimes tall poplar-wands stand white, their heads
Outmeasuring the distant hills. Sometimes
The ground has a deep greenness; sometimes brown
In stubble; and sometimes no ground at all,
For the close strength of crops that stand unreaped.
The water-plots are sometimes all the sun's,—
Sometimes quite green through shadows filling them,
Or islanded with growth of reeds,—or else
Masked in grey dust like the wide face o' the fields.
And still the swiftness lasts; that to our speed
The trees seem shaken like a press of spears.

There is some count of us:—folks travelling capped,
Priesthood, and lank hard-featured soldiery,
Females (no women), blouses, Hunt, and I.

We are relayed at Amiens. The steam
Snorts, chafes, and bridles, like three hundred horse,
And flings its dusky mane upon the air.
Our company is thinned, and lamps alight.
But still there are the folds in travelling-caps,
No priesthood now, but always soldiery,
And babies to make up for show in noise;
Females (no women), blouses, Hunt, and I.

Our windows at one side are shut for warmth;
Upon the other side, a leaden sky,
Hung in blank glare, makes all the country dim,

Which too seems bald and meagre, — be it truth,
Or of the waxing darkness. Here and there
The shade takes light, where in thin patches stand
The unstirred dregs of water.

Antwerp to Ghent

We are upon the Scheldt. We know we move
Because there is a floating at our eyes
Whatso they seek; and because all the things
Which on our outset were distinct and large
Are smaller and much weaker and quite grey,
And at last gone from us. No motion else.

We are upon the road. The thin swift moon
Runs with the running clouds that are the sky,
And with the running water runs—at whiles
Weak 'neath the film and heavy growth of reeds.
The country swims with motion. Time itself
Is consciously beside us, and perceived.
Our speed is such the sparks our engine leaves
Are burning after the whole train has passed.
The darkness is a tumult. We tear on,
The roll behind us and the cry before,
Constantly, in a lull of intense speed
And thunder. Any other sound is known
Merely by sight. The shrubs, the trees your eye
Scans for their growth, are far along in haze.
The sky has lost its clouds, and lies away
Oppressively at calm : the moon has failed :
Our speed has set the wind against us. Now
Our engine's heat is fiercer, and flings up
Great glares alongside. Wind and steam and speed
And clamour and the night. We are in Ghent.

DANTE GABRIEL ROSSETTI (1828–1882)

The railroad

Why! why to yon arch do the people drift,
Like a sea hurrying in to a cavern's rift,
Or like streams to a whirlpool streaming swift?
            'Tis the railroad!
Each street and each causeway endeth there;
And the whole of their peoples may step one stair
Down from the arch, and a power shall bear
Them swifter than wind from the mighty lair;
            'Tis the railroad!

Pass through the arch; put your ear to the ground!
This road sweepeth on through the isle and around!
You touch that which touches the country's bound!
            'Tis the railroad!
Like arrowy lightning snatch'd from the sky,
And bound to the earth, the bright rails lie;
And their way is straight driven through mountains
     high.
And headland to headland o'er valleys they tie;
            'Tis the railroad!

See how the engine hums still on the rails,
While his long train of cars slowly down to him sails;
He staggers like a brain blooded high, and he wails;
            'Tis the railroad!
His irons take the cars, and screaming he goes;
Now may heaven warn before him all friends and all
     foes!
A whole city's missives within him repose,
Half a thousand miles his, ere the day's hours close;
            'Tis the railroad!

EBENEZER JONES (1820–1860)

A railway reverie

from: All the Year Round (April 1862)

The dry tense cords against the signal-post
Rattle, like rigging of a wind-tossed ship;
And, overhead, up staring at the sun,
The scarlet target, duly split in half,
Silently tells that soon the gliding train,
Long-jointed, black, and winding, will glide in
With clamp, and roar, and hiss, and shrieking scream . . .

ANONYMOUS

The Meldon Viaduct, Devonshire. *From a photograph by R. Burnard*

There was a Young Lady of Sweden,
Who went by the slow train to Weedon;
   When they cried, 'Weedon Station!'
   She made no observation,
But she thought she should go back to Sweden.

EDWARD LEAR (1812–1888)

There was an Old Man at a Junction,
Whose feelings were wrung with compunction,
   When they said 'The Train's gone!'
   He exclaimed 'How forlorn!'
But remained on the rails of the Junction.

EDWARD LEAR (1812–1888)

The Express

After the first powerful plain manifesto,
The black statement of pistons, without more fuss
But gliding like a queen, she leaves the station.
Without bowing and with restrained unconcern
She passes the houses which humbly crowd outside,
The gasworks, and at last the heavy page
Of death, printed by gravestones in the cemetery.
Beyond the town there lies the open country
Where, gathering speed, she acquires mystery,
The luminous self-possession of ships on ocean.
It is now she begins to sing – at first quite low
Then loud, and at last with a jazzy madness –
The song of her whistle screaming at curves,
Of deafening tunnels, brakes, innumerable bolts.
And always light, aerial, underneath,
Retreats the elate metre of her wheels.
Steaming through metal landscape on her lines,
She plunges new eras of wild happiness,
Where speed throws up strange shapes, broad curves
And parallels clean like the steel of guns.
At last, further than Edinburgh or Rome,
Beyond the crest of the world, she reaches night
Where only a low stream-line brightness
Of phosphorus on the tossing hills is white.
Ah, like a comet through flame she moves entranced,
Wrapt in her music no bird song, no, nor bough
Breaking with honey buds, shall ever equal.

STEPHEN SPENDER (1909–   )

Illustrations by Edward Lear

Skimbleshanks: the railway cat

There's a whisper down the line at 11.39
When the Night Mail's ready to depart,
Saying 'Skimble where is Skimble has he gone to hunt the
      thimble?
We must find him or the train can't start.
All the guards and all the porters and the stationmaster's
      daughters
They are searching high and low,
Saying 'Skimble where is Skimble for unless he's very nimble
Then the Night Mail just can't go.'
At 11.42 then the signal's nearly due
And the passengers are frantic to a man—
Then Skimble will appear and he'll saunter to the rear:
He's been busy in the luggage van!
    He gives one flash of his glass-green eyes
        And the signal goes 'All Clear!'
    And we're off at last for the northern part
        Of the Northern Hemisphere!

You may say that by and large it is Skimble who's in charge
Of the Sleeping Car Express.
From the driver and the guards to the bagmen playing cards
He will supervise them all, more or less.
Down the corridor he paces and examines all the faces
Of the travellers in the First and in the Third;
He establishes control by a regular patrol
And he'd know at once if anything occurred.
He will watch you without winking and he sees what you are
      thinking
And it's certain that he doesn't approve
Of hilarity and riot, so the folk are very quiet
When Skimble is about and on the move.
    You can play no pranks with Skimbleshanks!
      He's a Cat that cannot be ignored;

So nothing goes wrong on the Northern Mail
    When Skimbleshanks is aboard.

Oh it's very pleasant when you have found your little den
With your name written up on the door.
And the berth is very neat with a newly folded sheet
And there's not a speck of dust on the floor.
There is every sort of light—you can make it dark or bright;
There's a handle that you turn to make a breeze.
There's a funny little basin you're suppose to wash your face in
And a crank to shut the window if you sneeze.
Then the guard looks in politely and will ask you very brightly
'Do you like your morning tea weak or strong?'
But Skimble's just behind him and was ready to remind him,
For Skimble won't let anything go wrong.
    And when you creep into your cosy berth
      And pull up the counterpane,
    You ought to reflect that it's very nice
    To know that you won't be bothered by mice—
    You can leave all that to the Railway Cat,
      The Cat of the Railway Train!

In the watches of the night he is always fresh and bright;
Every now and then he has a cup of tea
With perhaps a drop of Scotch while he's keeping on the watch,
Only stopping here and there to catch a flea,
You were fast asleep at Crewe and so you never knew
That he was walking up and down the station;
You were sleeping all the while he was busy at Carlisle,
Where he greets the stationmaster with elation.
But you saw him at Dumfries, where he speaks to the police
If there's anything they ought to know about:
When you get to Gallowgate there you do not have to wait—
For Skimbleshanks will help you to get out!
    He gives you a wave of his long brown tail
      Which says: 'I'll see you again!
    You'll meet without fail on the Midnight Mail
      The Cat of the Railway Train.'

T. S. ELIOT (1888–1965)

Out of the Window

In the middle of countries, far from hills and sea,
Are the little places one passes by in trains
And never stops at; where the skies extend
Uninterrupted, and the level plains
Stretch green and yellow and green without an end.
And behind the glass of their Grand Express
Folk yawn away a province through,
With nothing to think of, nothing to do,
Nothing even to look at—never a 'view'
In this damned wilderness.
But I look out of the window and find
Much to satisfy the mind.
Mark how the furrows, formed and wheeled
In a motion orderly and staid,
Sweep, as we pass, across the field
Like a drilled army on parade.
And here's a market-garden, barred
With stripe on stripe of varied greens . . .
Bright potatoes, flower starred,
And the opacous colour of beans.
Each line deliberately swings
Towards me, till I see a straight
Green avenue to the heart of things,
The glimpse of a sudden opened gate
Piercing the adverse walls of fate . . .
A moment only, and then, fast, fast,
The gate swings to, the avenue closes;
Fate laughs, and once more interposes
Its barriers.
        The train has passed.

ALDOUS HUXLEY (1894–1963)

The Nineteenth Century

Stockton to Darlington, 1825:
Stephenson on the sparkling iron road –
Chimney-hatted and frock-coated – drives
His locomotive, while the Lydian mode
Of Opus 132 may actually be
In the course of making. At twelve miles an hour
The century rushes to futurity,
Where art will be mankind-destroying power.
How can the music fail to bear the dates
And quirks of fashion time must prove
Grotesque? Especially as it celebrates
Avuncular and bust fraternal love.
Yet somehow an anachronistic god
Has lasted beyond his final period.

ROY FULLER (1912–   )

'The Rocket'

Railway superseded

from: The Testament of Sir Simon Simplex concerning Automobilism

That railways are inadequate appears
Indubitable now. For sixty years
Their comfort grew until the *train de luxe*
Arrived, arousing in conducted Cook's,
And other wholesale tourists, an envious smart,
For here they recognized the perfect art
And science of land-travel. Now we sing
A greater era, hail a happier Spring.
The motor-car reveals ineptitude
In railway-trains; and travellers conclude
The railway is archaic: strictly true,
Although the reason sounds as false as new:—
Railways are democratic, vulgar, laic;
And who can doubt Democracy's archaic?
The railway was the herald and the sign,
And powerful agent in the swift decline
Of Europe and the West. The future sage
Will blame sententiously the railway age,
Preachers upon its obvious vices pounce,
And poets, wits and journalists pronounce
The nineteenth century in prose and rhyme
The most unhappy period of time.

JOHN DAVIDSON (1857–1908)

'The Railway Station' *W.P. Frith*

Travel

The railroad track is miles away,
    And the day is loud with voices speaking,
Yet there isn't a train goes by all day
    But I hear its whistle shrieking.

All night there isn't a train goes by,
    Though the night is still for sleep and dreaming,
But I see its cinders red on the sky,
    And hear its engine steaming.

My heart is warm with the friends I make,
    And better friends I'll not be knowing,
Yet there isn't a train I wouldn't take,
    No matter where it's going.

EDNA ST. VINCENT MILLAY (1892–1950)

In the train

As we rush, as we rush in the Train,
    The trees and the houses go wheeling back,
But the starry heavens above the plain
    Come flying on our track.

All the beautiful stars of the sky,
    The silver doves of the forest of Night,
Over the dull earth swarm and fly,
    Companions of our flight.

We will rush ever on without fear;
    Let the goal be far, the flight be fleet!
For we carry the Heavens with us, dear,
    While the earth slips from our feet!

JAMES THOMPSON (1834–1882)

A local train of thought

Alone, in silence, at a certain time of night,
Listening, and looking up from what I'm trying to write,
I hear a local train along the Valley. And 'There
Goes the one-fifty', think I to myself; aware
That somehow its habitual travelling comforts me,
Making my world seem safer, homelier, sure to be
The same to-morrow; and the same, one hopes, next year.
'There's peacetime in that train.' One hears it disappear
With needless warning whistle and rail-resounding wheels.
'That train's quite like an old familiar friend', one feels.

SIEGFRIED SASSOON (1886–1967)

Through the tunnels

from: Aurora Leigh

                    So we passed
The liberal open country and the close,
And shot through tunnels, like a lightning-wedge
By great Thor-hammers driven through the rock,
Which, quivering through the intestine blackness, splits,
And lets it in at once: the train swept in
Athrob with effort, trembling with resolve,
The fierce denouncing whistle wailing on
And dying off smothered in the shuddering dark,
While we, self-awed, drew troubled breath, oppressed
As other Titans underneath the pile
And nightmare of the mountains. Out, at last,
To catch the dawn afloat upon the land!

ELIZABETH BARRETT BROWNING (1806–1861)

The wreck on the C. & O.

Along came the F.F.V., the fastest on the line,
Running o'er the C. & O. Road, twenty minutes behind the
    time;
Running into Sewell yard, was quartered on the line,
A-waiting for strict orders and in the cab to ride.

Chorus:
    Many a man has been murdered by the railroad, railroad,
        railroad,
    Many a man has been murdered by the railroad,
    And laid in his lonesome grave.

And when she blew for Hinton, her engineer was there,
George Alley was his name, with bright and wavery hair;
His fireman, Jack Dixon, was standing by his side,
A-waiting for strict orders and in the cab to ride.

George Alley's mother came to him with a basket on her arm,
She handed him a letter, saying: 'Be careful how you run;
And if you run your engine right, you'll get there just on time,
For many a man has lost his life in trying to make lost time.'

George Alley said: 'Dear mother, your letter I'll take heed.
I know my engine is all right and I know that she will speed;
So o'er this road I mean to run with speed unknown to all,
And when I blow for Clifton Forge, they'll surely hear my call.'

George Alley said to his fireman, 'Jack, a little extra steam;
I intend to run old No. 4 the fastest ever seen;
So o'er this road I mean to fly like angel's wings unfold,
And when I blow for the Big Bend Tunnel, they'll surely hear
    my call.'

George Alley said to his fireman, 'Jack, a rock ahead I see,
And I know that death is lurking there for to grab both you and
    me;
So from this cab, dear Jack, you leap, your darling life to save,
For I want you to be an engineer while I'm sleeping in my
    grave.'

'Oh, no, dear George! that will not do, I want to die with you.'
'Oh, no, no, dear Jack; that will not be, I'll die for you and me.'
So from the cab dear Jack did leap, ol' New River was running
    high,
And he kissed the hand of his darling George as No. 4 flew by.

So up the road she dashed; against the rock she crashed;
The engine turning over and the coaches they came last;
George Alley's head in the firebox lay, while the burning flames
    rolled o'er:
'I'm glad I was born an engineer, to die on the C. & O. Road.'

George Alley's mother came to him and in sorrow she did sigh,
When she looked upon her darling boy and saw that he must
    die.
'Too late, too late, dear mother! my doom is almost o'er,
And I know that God will let me in when I reach that golden
    shore.'

The Doctor said, 'Dear George, O darling boy, keep still;
Your life may yet be spared, if it be God's precious will.'
'Oh, no, dear Doc, that cannot be, I want to die so free,
I want to die on the engine I love, 143.'

The people came from miles around this engineer to see.
George Alley said, 'God bless you, friends, I am sure you will
    find me here.'
His face and head all covered with blood, his eyes you could not
    see,
And as he died he cried aloud, 'Oh, nearer, My God, to thee.'

ANONYMOUS

Journey by train

We flash across the level.
  We thunder thro' the bridges.
We bicker down the cuttings.
  We sway along the ridges.

A rush of streaming hedges,
  Of jostling lights and shadows,
Of hurtling, hurrying stations,
  Of racing woods and meadows.

We charge the tunnels headlong—
  The blackness roars and shatters.
We crash between embankments—
  The open spins and scatters.

We shake off the miles like water,
  We might carry a royal ransom;
And I think of her waiting, waiting,
  And long for a common hansom.

W. E. HENLEY (1849–1903)

Maidenhead Bridge

Underground

(*The porter speaks*)

A quarter of an hour to wait,
  And quite sufficient too,
Since your remarks on Bishopsgate
  Impress the mind as true,
Unless you work here soon and late,
  Till 'tis like home to you.

You see, a chap stands what he must,
  He'll hang on anywhere;
He'll learn to live on smoke and dust,
  Though 'tisn't healthy fare.
We're used to breathing grime in, just
  Like you to breathing air.

And yet 'tis odd to think these trains,
  In half an hour, maybe,
Will be right out among green lanes,
  Where the air is pure and free.
Well, sir, there's Bishopsgate remains
  For us, and here are we!

Your train. First class, sir. That's your style!
  In future, I'll be bound,
You'll stick to hansoms, since you'd spile
  Here in the Underground.
I've got to wait a little while
  Before *my* train comes round.

MAY KENDALL (1861–   )

The Kendal and Windermere Railway

Proud were ye, Mountains, when, in times of old,
Your patriot sons, to stem invasive war,
Intrenched your brows; ye gloried in each scar:
Now, for your shame, a Power, the Thirst of Gold,
That rules o'er Britain like a baneful star,
Wills that your peace, your beauty, shall be sold,
And clear way made for her triumphal car
Through the beloved retreats your arms enfold!
Hear YE that Whistle? As her long-linked Train
Swept onwards, did the vision cross your view?
Yes, ye were startled;—and, in balance true,
Weighing the mischief with the promised gain,
Mountains, and Vales, and Floods, I call on you
To share the passion of a just disdain.

WILLIAM WORDSWORTH (1770–1850)

'Rain, Steam and Speed. The Great Western Railway'. Detail J.M.W. Turner

Railway note

The station roofs curve off and line is lost
In white thick vapour. A smooth marble sun
Hangs there. It is the sun. An ermine frost
Edges each thorn and willow skeleton
Beyond the ghosts of goods-yard engines. Who
On earth will get the big expresses through?
But these men do.
We ride incredulous at the use and eyes
That pierce this blankness: like a sword-fish flies
The train with other trains ahead, behind,
Signalled with detonation, whistle, shout;
At the great junction stops.
Ticket-collectors board us and fling out
Their pleasantry as though
They liked things so,
Answering the talkative considerate kind,
'Not so bad now, but it's *been* bad you know.'

EDMUND BLUNDEN (1896–1974)

Gare St Lazare *Claude Monet*

The Train

from: Dombey and Son

Away, with a shriek, and a roar and a rattle, from the town,
burrowing among the dwellings of men and making the streets
hum, flashing out into the meadows for a moment, mining in
through the damp earth, booming on in darkness and heavy air,
bursting out again into the sunny day so bright and wide; away,
with a shriek, and a roar, and a rattle, through the fields,
through the woods, through the corn, through the hay,
through the chalk, through the mould, through the clay,
through the rock, among objects close at hand and almost in the
grasp, ever flying from the traveller, and a deceitful distance
ever moving slowly within him: like as in the track of the
remorseless monster, Death!

Through the hollow, on the height, by the heath, by the
orchard, by the park, by the garden, over the canal, across the
river, where the sheep are feeding, where the mill is going,
where the barge is floating, where the dead are lying, where the
factory is smoking, where the stream is running, where the
village clusters, where the cathedral rises, where the bleak moor
lies, and the wild breeze smooths or ruffles it at its inconstant
will: away, with a shriek, and a roar, and a rattle, and no trace to
leave behind but dust and vapour: like as in the track of the
remorseless monster, Death!

Breasting the wind and light, the shower and sunshine, away,
and still away, it rolls and roars, fierce and rapid, smooth and
certain, and great works and massive bridges crossing up above,
fall like a beam of shadow an inch broad, upon the eye, and then
are lost. Away, and still away, onward and onward ever:
glimpses of cottage-homes, of houses, mansions, rich estates, of
husbandry and handicraft, of people, of old roads and paths that
look deserted, small, and insignificant as they are left behind:
and so they do, and what else is there but such glimpses, in the
track of the indomitable monster, Death!

Away, with a shriek, and a roar, and a rattle, plunging down
into the earth again, and working on in such a storm of energy

'Canterbury from the South Eastern Railway'

and perseverance, that amidst the darkness and whirlwind the
motion seems reversed, and to tend furiously backward, until a
ray of light upon the wet walls shows its surface flying past like a
fierce stream. Away once more into the day, and through the
day, with a shrill yell of exultation, roaring, rattling, rearing on,
spurning everything with its dark breath, sometimes pausing
for a minute where a crowd of faces are, that in a minute more
are not: sometimes lapping water greedily, and before the spout
at which it drinks has ceased to drip upon the ground, shrieking,
roaring, rattling through the purple distance!

CHARLES DICKENS (1812–1870)

Limited

I am riding on a limited express, one of the crack trains of the
   nation.
Hurtling across the prairie into blue haze and dark air go fifteen
   all-steel coaches holding a thousand people.
(All the coaches shall be scrap and rust and all the men and
   women laughing in the diners and sleepers shall pass to
   ashes.)
I ask a man in the smoker where he is going and he answers:
   'Omaha.'

CARL SANDBURG (1878–1967)

I like to see it lap the miles

I like to see it lap the miles,
And lick the valleys up,
And stop to feed itself at tanks;
And then, prodigious, step

Around a pile of mountains,
And, supercilious, peer
In shanties by the sides of roads;
And then a quarry pare

To fit its sides, and crawl between,
Complaining all the while
In horrid, hooting stanza;
Then chase itself down hill

And neigh like Boanerges;
Then, punctual as a star,
Stop – docile and omnipotent –
At its own stable door.

EMILY DICKINSON (1830–1886)

'North Truro Station', Mass. *Edward Hopper*

The wreck of the six-wheel driver

Joseph Mickel was a good engineer,
Told his foreman, well, oh, not to fear.
All he wanted was to keep her good and hot.
Says, 'We'll make Paris 'bout four o'clock.'
Says, 'We'll make Paris 'bout four o'clock.'

When we got within a mile of the place,
Number One stared us all in the face.
The conductor pulled out his watch
And he mumbled and said,
'We may make it, but we'll all be dead.
All be dead, oh, we'll all be dead,
We may make it but we'll all be dead,
For I've been on the Charley so long.'

As the two locomotives was about to bump,
The foreman prepared for to make his jump.
The engineer blowed the whistle
And the foreman bawled,
'Please, Mr. Conductor, won't you save us all,
Save us all, oh, save us all,
Please, Mr. Conductor, won't you save us all?
For I've been on the Charley so long.'

Oh, you ought to been there for to have seen the sight,
Screaming and yelling, both colored and white.
Some were crippled, and some were *lame*;
But the six-wheel driver had to bear the blame.
Ain't it a pity, oh, ain't it a shame
That the six wheel driver had to bear the blame?
For I've been on the Charley so long.

ANONYMOUS

'Manchester Valley', New Hope, Pennsylvania. *Joseph Pickett*

'The Dining Car'. *Victor Pasmore*

Restaurant car

Fondling only to throttle the nuzzling moment
Smuggled under the table, hungry or not
We roughride over the sleepers, finger the menu,
Avoid our neighbours' eyes and wonder what

Mad country moves beyond the steamed-up window
So fast into the past we could not keep
Our feet on it one instant. Soup or grapefruit?
We had better eat to pass the time, then sleep

To pass the time. The water in the carafe
Shakes its hips, both glass and soup plate spill,
The tomtom beats in the skull, the waiters totter
Along their invisible tightrope. For good or ill,

For fish or meat, with single tickets only,
Our journey still in the nature of a surprise,
Could we, before we stop where all must change,
Take one first risk and catch our neighbours' eyes?

LOUIS MACNEICE (1907–1963)

52

Night Mail

This is the night mail crossing the border,
Bringing the cheque and the postal order,
Letters for the rich, letters for the poor,
The shop at the corner and the girl next door.
Pulling up Beattock, a steady climb –
The gradient's against her, but she's on time.

Past cotton grass and moorland boulder,
Shovelling white steam over her shoulder,
Snorting noisily as she passes
Silent miles of wind-bent grasses.
Birds turn their heads as she approaches,
Stare from the bushes at her blank-faced coaches.
Sheepdogs cannot turn her course,
They slumber on with paws across.
In the farm she passes no one wakes,
But a jug in the bedroom gently shakes.

Dawn freshens, the climb is done.
Down towards Glasgow she descends
Towards the steam tugs yelping down the glade of cranes,
Towards the fields of apparatus, the furnaces
Set ōn the dark plain like gigantic chessmen.
All Scotland waits for her:
In the dark glens, beside the pale-green lochs,
Men long for news.

Letters of thanks, letters from banks,
Letters of joy from girl and boy,
Receipted bills, and invitations
To inspect new stock or visit relations,
And applications for situations
And timid lovers' declarations
And gossip, gossip from all the nations,

News circumstantial, news financial,
Letters with holiday snaps to enlarge in,
Letters with faces scrawled in the margin,
Letters from uncles, cousins and aunts,
Letters to Scotland from the South of France,
Letters of condolence to Highlands and Lowlands,
Notes from overseas to Hebrides
Written on paper of every hue,
The pink, the violet, the white and the blue,
The chatty, the catty, the boring, adoring,
The cold and official and the heart's outpouring,
Clever, stupid, short and long,
The typed and the printed and the spelt all wrong.

Thousands are still asleep
Dreaming of terrifying monsters,
Or a friendly tea beside the band at Cranston's or Crawford's,
Asleep in working Glasgow, asleep in well-set Edinburgh,
Asleep in granite Aberdeen.
They continue their dreams;
But shall wake soon and long for letters,
And none will hear the postman's knock
Without a quickening of the heart,
For who can hear and feel himself forgotten?

W. H. AUDEN (1907–1973)

The Underground

from: Summoned by Bells

... There was no station, north to Finsbury Park,
To Barking eastwards, Clapham Common south,
No temporary platform in the west
Among the Actons and the Ealings, where
We had not once alighted. Metroland
Beckoned us out to lanes in beechy Bucks –
Goldschmidt and Howland (in a wooden hut
Besides the station): 'Most attractive sites
Ripe for development'; Charrington's for coal;
And not far off the neo-Tudor shops.
We knew the different railways by their smells.
The City and South reeked like a changing-room;
Its orange engines and old rolling-stock,
Its narrow platforms, undulating tracks,
Seemed even then historic. Next in age,
The Central London, with its cut-glass shades
On draughty stations, had an ozone smell –
Not seaweed-scented ozone from the sea
But something chemical from Birmingham. ...

JOHN BETJEMAN (1906–   )

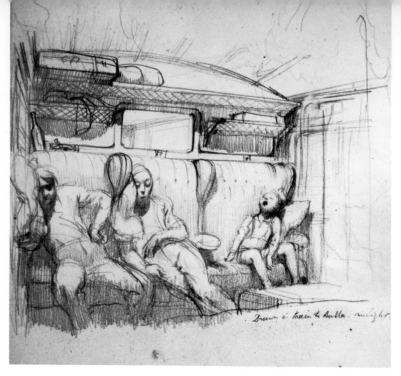

'In the Train to Aulla, midnight', *Rex Whistler*

Dawn

Opposite me two Germans snore and sweat.
   Through sullen swirling gloom we jolt and roar.
We have been here for ever: even yet
   A dim watch tells two hours, two aeons, more.
The windows are tight-shut and slimy-wet
   With a night's foetor. There are two hours more;
Two hours to dawn and Milan; two hours yet.
   Opposite me two Germans sweat and snore. . . .

One of them wakes, and spits, and sleeps again.
The darkness shivers. A wan light through the rain
Strikes on our faces, drawn and white. Somewhere
A new day sprawls; and, inside, the foul air
Is chill, and damp, and fouler than before. . . .
Opposite me two Germans sweat and snore.

RUPERT BROOKE (1887–1915)

Adlestrop

Yes. I remember Adlestrop –
The name, because one afternoon
Of heat the express-train drew up there
Unwontedly. It was late June.

The steam hissed. Someone cleared his throat.
No one left and no one came
On the bare platform. What I saw
Was Adlestrop – only the name

And willows, willow-herb, and grass,
And meadowsweet, and haycocks dry,
No whit less still and lonely fair
Than the high cloudlets in the sky.

And for that minute a blackbird sang
Close by, and round him, mistier,
Farther and farther, all the birds
Of Oxfordshire and Gloucestershire.

EDWARD THOMAS (1878–1917)

Lordship Lane Station, 1871. *Camille Pissarro*

The arriving train

(*Dartmouth Arms Station : Croydon Railway,
April 28th, 1844.*)

Behold, smoke-panoplied, the wondrous car!
  Strong and impetuous, but obedient still;
Behold it comes, loud panting from afar,
  As if it lived, and of its own fierce will
  Ran a free race with wild winds blowing shrill!
Fire-bowell'd, iron-ribb'd, of giant length
Snake-like, it comes exulting in its strength,
  The pride of art – the paragon of skill!
Triumph of mind! what hand thy bound shall mark?
  Lo! through the curtain of the coming time,
Seen looming palpably 'mid cloud and dark,
  Yet other triumphs, more than this sublime,
Rise numerous on the far-seeing ken
Of those who watch, and hope the good of men.

CHARLES MACKAY (1814–1889)

The *James Toleman*, 1892

Faintheart in a railway train

At nine in the morning there passed a church,
At ten there passed me by the sea,
At twelve a town of smoke and smirch,
At two a forest of oak and birch,
   And then, on a platform, she:

A radiant stranger, who saw not me.
I said, 'Get out to her do I dare?'
But I kept my seat in my search for a plea,
And the wheels move on. O could it but be
   That I had alighted there!

THOMAS HARDY (1840–1928)

'Waiting for the Train'. *J.H. Tissot*

This train

This train is bound for glory, this train,
This train is bound for glory, this train,
This train is bound for glory,
If you ride in it, you must be holy, this train.

This train don' pull no extras, this train,
Don' pull nothin' but de Midnight Special.

This train don' pull no sleepers, this train,
Don' pull nothin' but the righteous people, this train.

This train don' pull no jokers, this train,
Neither don' pull no cigar smokers, this train.

This train is bound for glory, this train.
If you ride in it, you mus' be holy, this train.

ANONYMOUS

'American Express Train'. *Currier and Ives lithograph after F. E. Palmer*

Sleeping compartment

I don't like this, being carried sideways
Through the night. I feel wrong and helpless – like
A timber broadside in a fast stream.

Such a way of moving may suit
That odd snake the sidewinder
In Arizona: but not me in Perthshire.

I feel at rightangles to everything,
A crossgrain in existence. – It scrapes
The top of my head, my footsoles.

To forget outside is no help either –
Then I become a blockage
In the long gut of the train.

I try to think I am a through-the-looking-glass
Mountaineer bivouacked
On a ledge five feet high.

It's no good. I go sidelong.
I rock sideways. . . . I draw in my feet
To let Aviemore pass.

NORMAN MACCAIG (1910–   )

Morning express

Along the wind-swept platform, pinched and white,
The travellers stand in pools of wintry light,
Offering themselves to morn's long, slanting arrows,
The train's due; porters trundle laden barrows.
The train steams in, volleying resplendent clouds
    Of sun-blown vapour. Hither and about,
Scared people hurry, storming the doors in crowds.
    The officials seem to waken with a shout,
Resolved to hoist and plunder; some to the vans
Leap; others rumble the milk in gleaming cans.
Boys, indolent-eyed, from baskets leaning back,
    Question each face; a man with a hammer steals
Stooping from coach to coach; with clang and clack
    Touches and tests, and listens to the wheels.
Guard sounds a warning whistle, points to the clock
With brandished flag, and on his folded flock
Claps the last door: the monster grunts: 'Enough!'
Tightening his load of links with pant and puff.
Under the arch, then forth into blue day,
Glide the processional windows on their way,
And glimpse the stately folk who sit at ease
To view the world like kings taking the seas
In prosperous weather: drifting banners tell
    Their progress to the counties; with them goes
    The clamour of their journeying; while those
Who sped them stand to wave a last farewell.

SIEGFRIED SASSOON (1886–1967)

Liverpool Street station

Through crystal roofs the sunlight fell,
And pencilled beams the gloss renewed
On iron rafters balanced well
On iron struts; though dimly hued,
With smoke o'erlaid, with dust endued,
The walls and beams like beryl shone;
And dappled light the platforms strewed
With yellow foliage of the dawn
That withered by the porch of day's divan.

The fragrant, suave autumnal air
A dulcet Indian summer breathed,
Able to reach the inmost lair
Unclean of London's interwreathed
And labyrinthine railways; sheathed
In annual increments of soot:
Memories of regions parked and heathed,
Of orchards lit with golden fruit
Attuned October's subterranean lute.

But orchards lit with golden lamps,
Or purple moor, or nutbrown stream,
Or mountains where the morn encamps
Frequent no station-loafer's dream:
A breed of folk forlorn that seem
The heirs of disappointment, cast
By fate to be the preacher's theme,
To hunger daily and to fast,
And sink to helpless indigence at last.

'Arrival of Christmas Train, Eastern Counties Railway'

From early morn they hang about
The bookstall, the refreshment room;
They pause and think, as if in doubt
Which train to go by; now assume
A jaunty air, and now in gloom
They take the platform for a stage
And pace it, meditating doom –
Their own, the world's; in baffled rage
Condemning still the imperceptive age.

JOHN DAVIDSON (1857–1908)

Casey Jones

Come all you rounders for I want you to hear
The story of a brave engineer;
Casey Jones was the fellow's name,
A big eight-wheeler of a mighty fame.
Caller called Casey at half-past four,
He kissed his wife at the station door,
Mounted to the cabin with orders in his hand,
And took his farewell trip to the promised land.
    Casey Jones, he mounted to the cabin,
    Casey Jones, with his orders in his hand!
    Casey Jones, he mounted to the cabin,
    Took his farewell trip into the promised land.

Put in your water and shovel in your coal,
Put your head out the window, watch the drivers roll,
I'll run her till she leaves the rail,
'Cause we're eight hours late with the Western Mail!
He looked at his watch and his watch was slow,
Looked at the water and the water was low,
Turned to his fireboy and said,
'We'll get to 'Frisco, but we'll all be dead!'
    Chorus

Casey pulled up Reno Hill,
Tooted for the crossing with an awful shrill,
Snakes all knew by the engine's moans
That the hogger at the throttle was Casey Jones.
He pulled up short two miles from the place,
Number Four stared him right in the face,
Turned to his fireboy, said 'You'd better jump,
'Cause there's two locomotives going to bump!'
    Chorus

'American Railroad Scene', 1874: *From a Currier and Ives lithograph*

Casey said, just before he died,
'There's two more roads I'd like to ride.'
Fireboy said, 'What can they be?'
'The Rio Grande and the Old S.P.'
Mrs. Jones sat on her bed a-sighing,
Got a pink that Casey was dying,
Said, 'Go to bed, children; hush your crying,
'Cause you'll get another papa on the Salt Lake line.'
    Casey Jones! Got another papa!
    Casey Jones, on the Salt Lake Line!
    Casey Jones! Got another papa!
    Got another papa on the Salt Lake Line!

WALLACE SAUNDERS

The Euston terminus

Railways 1846

'No poetry in Railways!' foolish thought
Of a dull brain, to no fine music wrought.
By mammon dazzled, though the people prize
The gold alone, yet shall not we despise
The triumphs of our time, or fail to see
Of pregnant mind the fruitful progeny
Ushering the daylight of the world's new morn.
Look up, ye doubters, be no more forlorn!—
Smooth your rough brows, ye little wise: rejoice,
Ye who despond: and with exulting voice
Salute, ye earnest spirits of our time,
The young Improvement ripening to her prime,
Who, in the fulness of her genial youth,
Prepares the way for Liberty and Truth,
And breaks the barriers that, since earth began,
Have made mankind the enemy of man.

Lay down your rails, ye nations, near and far—
Yoke your full trains to Steam's triumphal car;
Link town to town; unite in iron bands
The long-estranged and oft-embattled lands . . .

  Blessings on Science, and her handmaid Steam!
They make Utopia only half a dream;
And show the fervent, of capacious souls,
Who watch the ball of Progress as it rolls,
That all as yet completed, or begun,
Is but the dawning that precedes the sun.

CHARLES MACKAY (1814–1889)

The branch line

Professing loud energy, out of the junction departed
The branch-line engine. The small train rounded the bend
Watched by us pilgrims of summer, and most by me, —
Who had known this picture since first my travelling started,
And knew it as sadly pleasant, the usual end
Of singing returns to beloved simplicity.

The small train went from view behind the plantation,
Monotonous, — but there's a grace in monotony!
I felt its journey, I watched in imagination
Its brown smoke spun with sunshine wandering free
Past the great weir with its round flood-mirror beneath,
And where the magpie rises from orchard shadows,
And among the oasts, and like a rosy wreath
Mimicking children's flower-play in the meadows.

The thing so easy, so daily, of so small stature
Gave me another picture: of war's warped face
Where still the sun and the leaf and the lark praised Nature,
But no little engine bustled from place to place;
When summer succeeded summer, yet only ghosts
Or to-morrow's ghosts could venture hand or foot
In the track between the terrible telegraph-posts, —
The end of all things lying between the hut
Which lurked this side, and the shattered local train
That.
    So easy it was; and should that come again—.

EDMUND BLUNDEN (1896–1974)

A railroad eclogue

Father What brought thee back, lad?
Son   Father! the same feet
       As took me brought me back, I warrant ye.
Father Couldst thou not find the rail?
Son   The deuce himself
       Who can find most things, could not find the rail.
Father Plain as a pike-staff miles and miles it lies.
Son   So they all told me. Pike-staffs in your day
       Must have been hugely plainer than just now.
Father What didst thou ask for?
Son   Ask for? Tewkesbury
       Thro' Defford opposite to Breedon-hill.
Father Right: and they set ye wrong?
Son   Me wrong? not they;
       The best among 'em should not set me wrong,
       Nor right, nor anything; I'd tell 'em that.—
Father Herefordshire's short horns and shorter wits
       Are known in every quarter of the land,
       Those blunt, these blunter. Well! no help for it!
       Each might do harm if each had more of each . . .
       Yet even in Herefordshire there are some
       Not downright dolts . . . before the cidar's broacht,
       When all are much alike . . . yet most could tell
       A railroad from a parish or a pike.
       How thou couldst miss that railroad puzzles me,
       Seeing there lies none other round about.
Son   I found the rails along the whole brook-side
       Left of that old stone bridge across yon Avon.
Father That is the place.
Son   There was a house hard-by,
       And past it ran a furnace upon wheels,
       Like a mad bull, tail up in air, and horns
       So low ye might not see 'em. On it bumpt,
       Roaring, as strait as any arrow flits,

As strait, as fast too, ay, and faster went it,
And, could it keep its wind up and not crack,
Then woe betide the eggs at Tewkesbury
This market-day, and lambs, and sheep! a score
Of pigs might be made flitches in a trice,
Before they well could knuckle.
                              Father! father!
If they were ourn, thou wouldst not chuckle so,
And shake thy sides, and wipe thy eyes, and rub
Thy breeches-knees, like Sunday shoes, at that rate.
Hows'ever . . .

Father   'Twas the train, lad, 'twas the train.
Son   May-be: I had no business with a train.
         '*Go thee by rail*, you told me; *by the rail*
         At Defford . . .' and didst make a fool of me.
Father Ay, lad, I did indeed: it was methinks
         Some twenty years agone last Martinmas.

WALTER SAVAGE LANDOR (1775–1864)

Locomotive

He has a giant's frame,
He weighs ten thousand pounds of blackness,
His body is measured out . . . his every inch,
His pipes and wheels and countless nuts and bolts are
    rubbed and polished inside and out.
When he moves
The hands of meters are quick to turn;
When he runs
The rails and the sleepers shake;
And when his piston-arms begin to stretch,
When they shuffle to and fro and spin the wheels,
And when I see him sweep through towns and villages,
My heart starts throbbing,
Tears fill my eyes . . .
With a brass plate at his front
And a red lamp hanging out,
He is always emerging out of smoke, carrying a thousand lives.

Flags and signals
Wave him on . . . on shining rails in perfect order . . .
To the back of this big and honest man
We raise our arms in eager praise.

SHIGEHARU NAKANO
(*Translated from the Japanese by Takamichi Ninomiya and
    D. J. Enright*)

The Great Western Royal Train at St Mary Cray

From a railway carriage

Faster than fairies, faster than witches,
Bridges and houses, hedges and ditches;
And charging along like troops in a battle,
All through the meadows the houses and cattle;
And all of the sights of the hill and the plain
Fly as thick as driving rain;
And ever again, in the wink of an eye,
Painted stations whistle by.

Here is a child who clambers and scrambles,
All by himself and gathering brambles;
Here is a tramp who stands and gazes;
And here is the green for stringing the daisies!
Here is a cart run away in the road
Lumping along with man and load;
And here is a mill, and there is a river;
Each a glimpse and gone for ever!

ROBERT LOUIS STEVENSON (1850–1894)

Charley Snyder

Charley Snyder was a good engineer,
He told his firemen he had nothing to fear,
All he needed was water and coal,
Put your head out the window, see the drivers roll,
    See the drivers roll,
    See the drivers roll,
Put your head out the window, see the drivers roll.

On Sunday morning it began to rain,
When around the bend came a passenger train,
On the bumpers was a hobo John,
He's a good old hobo, but he's dead and gone,
    He's dead and gone,
    He's dead and gone,
He's a good old hobo, but he's dead and gone.

Jay Gould's daughter said before she died,
'Father, fix the "blind" so the bums can't ride,
If ride they must, let them ride the rod,
Let them put their trust in the hands of God,
        In the hands of God,
        In the hands of God,
Let them put their trust in the hands of God.'

Jay Gould's daughter said before she died,
'There's just one more road o'er which I'd like to ride.'
'Tell me, daughter, what can it be?'
'It's in southern California on the Santa Fe,
        On the Santa Fe,
        On the Santa Fe.
It's in southern California on the Santa Fe.'

Hurry up, engine, and hurry up, train,
Missie gwine to ride over the road again,
Swift as lightning and smooth as glass,
Darkey, take your hat off when the train goes past,
        When the train goes past,
        When the train goes past,
Darkey, take your hat off when the train goes past.

ANONYMOUS

Train to Dublin

Our half-thought thoughts divide in sifted wisps
Against the basic facts repatterned without pause,
I can no more gather my mind up in my fist
Than the shadow of the smoke of this train upon the grass—
This is the way that animals' lives pass.

The train's rhythm never relents, the telephone posts
Go striding backwards like the legs of time to where
In a Georgian house you turn at the carpet's edge
Turning a sentence while, outside my window here,
The smoke makes broken queries in the air.

The train keeps moving and the rain holds off,
I count the buttons on the seat, I hear a shell
Held hollow to the ear, the mere
Reiteration of integers, the bell
That tolls and tolls, the monotony of fear.

At times we are doctrinaire, at times we are frivolous,
Plastering over the cracks, a gesture making good,
But the strength of us does not come out of us.
It is we, I think, are the idols and it is God
Has set us up as men who are painted wood,

And the trains carry us about. But not consistently so,
For during a tiny portion of our lives we are not in trains,
The idol living for a moment, not muscle-bound
But walking freely through the slanting rain,
Its ankles wet, its grimace relaxed again.

All over the world people are toasting the King,
Red lozenges of light as each one lifts his glass,
But I will not give you any idol or idea, creed or king,
I give you the incidental things which pass
Outward through space exactly as each was.

I give you the disproportion between labour spent
And joy at random; the laughter of the Galway sea
Juggling with spars and bones irresponsibly,
I give you the toy Liffey and the vast gulls,
I give you fuchsia hedges and whitewashed walls.

I give you the smell of Norman stone, the squelch
Of bog beneath your boots, the red bog-grass,
The vivid chequer of the Antrim hills, the trough of dark
Golden water for the cart-horses, the brass
Belt of serene sun upon the lough.

And I give you the faces, not the permanent masks,
But the faces balanced in the toppling wave—
His glint of joy in cunning as the farmer asks
Twenty per cent too much, or a girl's, forgetting to be suave,
A tiro choosing stuffs, preferring mauve.

And I give you the sea and yet again the sea's
Tumultuous marble,
With Thor's thunder of taking his ease akimbo,
Lumbering torso, but finger-tips a marvel
Of surgeon's accuracy.

I would like to give you more but I cannot hold
This stuff within my hands and the train goes on;
I know that there are further syntheses to which,
As you have perhaps, people at last attain
And find that they are rich and breathing gold.

LOUIS MACNEICE (1907–1963)

The L

from: The Tunnel

Or can't you quite make up your mind to ride;
A walk is better underneath the L a brisk
Ten blocks or so before? But you find yourself
Preparing penguin flexions of the arms,—
As usual you will meet the scuttle yawn:
The subway yawns the quickest promise home.

Be minimum, then, to swim the hiving swarms
Out of the Square, the Circle burning bright—
Avoid the glass doors gyring at your right,
Where boxed alone a second, eyes take fright
—Quite unprepared rush naked back to light:
And down beside the turnstile press the coin
Into the slot. The gongs already rattle.

> And so
> of cities you bespeak
> subways, rivered under streets
> and rivers . . . In the car
> the overtone of motion
> underground, the monotone
> of motion is the sound
> of other faces, also underground—

    ★   ★   ★

Whose head is swinging from the swollen strap?
Whose body smokes along the bitten rails,
Bursts from a smoldering bundle far behind
In back forks of the chasms of the brain,—
Puffs from a riven stump far out behind
In interborough fissures of the mind . . . ?
And why do I often meet your visage here,
Your eyes like agate lanterns—on and on
Below the toothpaste and the dandruff ads?
—And did their riding eyes right through your side,

New York Elevated Railway *an engraving after J.R. Brawn*

And did their eyes like unwashed platters ride?
And Death, aloft,—gigantically down
Probing through you—toward me, O evermore!
And when they dragged your retching flesh,
Your trembling hands that night through Baltimore—
That last night on the ballot rounds, did you
Shaking, did you deny the ticket, Poe?

For Gravesend Manor change at Chambers Street.
The platform hurries along to a dead stop.

HART CRANE (1899–1932)

The Newport railway

Success to the Newport Railway,
Along the braes of the Silvery Tay,
And to Dundee straightway,
Across the Railway Bridge o' the Silvery Tay,
Which was opened on the 12th of May,
In the year of our Lord 1879,
Which will clear all expenses in a very short time;
Because the thrifty housewives of Newport
To Dundee will often resort,
Which will be to them profit and sport,
By bringing cheap tea, bread, and jam,
And also some of Lipton's ham,
Which will make their hearts feel light and gay,
And cause them to bless the opening day
Of the Newport Railway.

The train is most beautiful to be seen,
With its long, white curling cloud of steam,
As the train passes on her way
Along the bonnie braes o' the Silvery Tay.

And if the people of Dundee
Should feel inclined to have a spree,
I am sure 'twill fill their hearts with glee
By crossing o'er to Newport,
And there they can have excellent sport,
By viewing the scenery beautiful and gay,
During the livelong summer day,

And then they can return at night
With spirits light and gay,
By the Newport Railway,
By night or by day,
Across the Railway Bridge o' the Silvery Tay.

Success to the undertakers of the Newport Railway
Hoping the Lord will their labours repay,
And prove a blessing to the people
For many a long day
Who live near by Newport,
On the bonnie braes o' the Silvery Tay.

WILLIAM MCGONAGALL (1830–1902)

Paddington Station. *Myles Birket Foster*

Oh! Mr Porter

Lately I just spent a week with my old Aunt Brown,
Came up to see the wond'rous sight of famous London Town. —
Just a week I had of it, all round the place we'd roam, —
Wasn't I sorry on the day I had to go back home? —
Worried about with packing I arrived late at the station,
Dropped my hat-box in the mud, the things all fell about, —
Got my ticket, said good-bye: 'Right away!' the guard did cry,
But I found the train was wrong, and shouted out: —

> *Chorus*
> Oh! Mister Porter, what shall I do! — —
> I want to go to Birmingham and they're taking me on to Crewe,
> Send me back to London as quickly as you can, —
> Oh! Mister Porter, what a silly girl I am.

The porter would not stop the train, but laughed and said, 'You must
    Keep your hair on, Mary Ann, and mind that you don't bust!'
Some old gentleman inside declared that it was hard, —
Said 'Look out of the window, Miss, and try and call the guard.'
Didn't I, too, with all my might I nearly balanced over,
But my old friend grasp'd my leg, and pulled me back again, —
Nearly fainting with the fright, I sank into his arms a sight,
Went into hysterics but I cried in vain: —
> *Chorus*

On his clean old shirt-front then I laid my trembling head,
'Do take it easy, rest a-while' the dear old chappie said. —
'If you make a fuss of me and on me do not frown, —
You shall have my mansion, dear, away in London Town!'
Wouldn't you think me silly if I said I could not like him?
Really seemed a nice old boy, so I replied this way; —
'I will be your own for life, your im-ay doodle-um little wife,
If you'll never tease me any more I say.' —
> *Chorus*

THOMAS LE BRUNN

On the departure platform

We kissed at the barrier; and passing through
She left me, and the moment by moment got
Smaller and smaller, until to my view
    She was but a spot;

A wee white spot of muslin fluff
That down the diminishing platform bore
Through hustling crowds of gentle and rough
    To the carriage door.

Under the lamplight's fitful glowers,
Behind dark groups from far and near,
Whose interests were apart from ours,
    She would disappear,

Then show again, till I ceased to see
That flexible form, that nebulous white;
And she who was more than my life to me
    Had vanished quite. . . .

We have penned new plans since that fair fond day,
And in season she will appear again—
Perhaps in the same soft white array—
    But never as then!

—'And why, young man, must eternally fly
A joy you'll repeat, if you love her well?'
—O friend, nought happens twice thus; why,
    I cannot tell!

THOMAS HARDY (1840–1928)

The Metropolitan Railway

Early Electric! With what radiant hope
   Men formed this many-branched electrolier,
Twisted the flex around the iron rope
   And let the dazzling vacuum globes hang clear,
And then with hearts the rich contrivance fill'd
O copper, beaten by the Bromsgrove Guild.

Early Electric! Sit you down and see,
   'Mid this fine woodwork and a smell of dinner,
A stained-glass windmill and a pot of tea,
   And sepia views of leafy lanes in PINNER,—
Then visualise, far down the shining lines,
Your parents' homestead set in murmuring pines.

Smoothly from HARROW, passing PRESTON ROAD,
   They saw the last green fields and misty sky,
At NEASDEN watched a workmen's train unload,
   And, with the morning villas sliding by,
They felt so sure on their electric trip
That Youth and Progress were in partnership.

And all that day in murky London Wall
    The thought of RUISLIP kept him warm inside;
At FARRINGDON that lunch hour at a stall
    He bought a dozen plants of London Pride;
While she, in arc-lit Oxford Street adrift
Soared through the sales by safe hydraulic lift.

Early Electric! Maybe even here
    They met that evening at six-fifteen
Beneath the hearts of this electrolier
    And caught the first non-stop to WILLESDEN GREEN,
Then out and on, through rural RAYNER'S LANE
To autumn-scented Middlesex again.

Cancer has killed him. Heart is killing her.
    The trees are down. An Odeon flashes fire
Where stood their villa by the murmuring fir
    When 'they would for their children's good conspire,'
Of all their loves and hopes on hurrying feet
Thou art the worn memorial, Baker Street.

JOHN BETJEMAN (1906–   )

London and Birmingham Railway, *c.* 1840

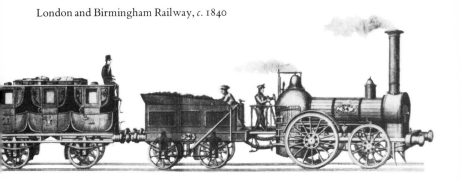

Acknowledgments

The Editor would like to thank the following for permission to reproduce certain copyright poems:

W. H. Auden, *Night Mail*, from COLLECTED SHORTER POEMS. Reprinted by permission of Faber and Faber Ltd.

Sir John Betjeman, *The Underground*, from SUMMONED BY BELLS, and *The Metropolitan Railway*, from COMPLETE POEMS. Reproduced by permission of John Murray (Publishers) Ltd.

Edmund Blunden, *Railway Note* and *The Branch Line*. Reprinted by permission of A. D. Peters & Co. Ltd.

T. S. Eliot, *Skimbleshanks*, from OLD POSSUM'S BOOK OF PRACTICAL CATS. Reprinted by permission of Faber and Faber Ltd.

Roy Fuller, *The Nineteenth Century*. Reprinted by permission of the Author.

Aldous Huxley, *Out of the Window*, from THE COLLECTED POEMS OF ALDOUS HUXLEY. Reprinted by permission of Mrs. Laura Huxley and Chatto & Windus Ltd.

Thomas Le Brunn, *Oh! Mr. Porter* C. George Le Brunn. A. Thomas Le Brunn. Copyright © 1893 Howard and Crew, assigned to Ascherberg Hopwood & Crew Ltd. Reproduced by permission of Ascherberg Hopwood & Crew Ltd.

Norman MacCaig, *The Sleeping Compartment*, from RINGS ON A TREE. Reprinted by permission of Norman MacCaig and The Hogarth Press.

Hart Crane, *The Tunnel*, from THE COLLECTED POEMS AND SELECTED LETTERS AND PROSE OF HART CRANE. Reprinted by permission of the Oxford University Press and Liveright Publishing Corporation.

Louis MacNeice, *Restaurant Car* and *Train to Dublin*, from THE COLLECTED POEMS OF LOUIS MACNEICE. Reprinted by permission of Faber and Faber Ltd.

Edna St Vincent Millay, *Travel*, from COLLECTED POEMS, Harper and Row. Copyright 1921, 1948 by Edna St Vincent Millay.

Harold Munro, *Journey*, from COLLECTED POEMS. Duckworth and Co. Ltd.

Shigeharu Nakano, *Locomotive* (translated by D. J. Enright), from THE POETRY OF LIVING IN JAPAN by Takamichi Ninomiya and D. J. Enright. Reprinted by permission of Bolt and Watson Ltd.

Carl Sandburg, *Limited*, from CHICAGO POEMS by Carl Sandburg, copyright 1916 by Holt, Rinehart and Winston Inc.; copyright © 1944 by Carl Sandburg. Reprinted by permission of Harcourt Brace Jovanovich Inc.

Siegfried Sassoon, *A Local Train of Thought* and *Morning Express*. Reprinted by permission of G. T. Sassoon, Esq.

Stephen Spender, *The Express*, from COLLECTED POEMS. Reprinted by permission of Faber and Faber Ltd.

The American railroad ballads, *The Wreck of the C. & O.* or *The Death of Jack Hilton*, *Charley Snyder* and *The Wreck of the Six-Wheel Driver* were collected, adapted and arranged by John A. Lomax and Alan Lomax. TRO – © Copyright 1934 and renewed 1962 Ludlow Music, Inc. By permission of TRO Essex Music Ltd, 19/20 Poland Street, London, W.1.